THE OFFICIAL DANCEHALL DICTIONARY

A Guide to Jamaican Dialect
and
Dancehall Slang

Researched and Compiled

by

Chester Francis-Jackson

© 1995 by Chester Francis-Jackson
Reprint 2002
Reprint 2004
Reprint 2009

Cover and Illustrations by Patrick Foster
Typeset in 11/13 Times by Lazertec Ltd.

Published by: LMH Publishing Limited
Suite 10-11
Sagicor Industrial Park
7 Norman Road
Kingston C.S.O., Jamaica
Tel.: 876-938-0005
Fax: 876-759-8752
Email: lmhbookpublishing@cwjamaica.com
Website: www.lmhpublishing.com

Printed in China   ISBN:976-610-154-X

TABLE OF CONTENTS

ACKNOWLEDGEMENTS

I would like to use this medium to convey special thanks to the following people:

Cherise Francis, Dale Williams, Patrick D. Bailey, Betty Delfosse and Sydney O. Murray for their invaluable contribution to the realization of the 'Dictionary'.

CHESTER FRANCIS-JACKSON

PREFACE

The development of Reggae music has been and continues to be an evolutionary process, creating its own trends – in fashion, in movement – and its own colourful language.

The music came out of the urban Jamaican ghettoes in the early 1960s and went on to secure its place on the international music stage with the pioneering efforts of artistes and groups such as Bob Marley, Jimmy Cliff, Toots Hibbert, Dennis Brown, Freddie McGregor, Gregory Issacs, Peter Tosh, Third World, The I Threes, Sly Dunbar and Robbie Shakespeare – 'The Rhythm Section' – and a host of other contributors. While essentially maintaining its Afro-Caribbean beat since its inception, the lyrical content of the "sound" has been steadily drifting away from being protest music or from the inspirational and the romantic themes of an earlier era, to becoming an instant commentary on current happenings.

Social commentary has always been one of the mainstays of the lyrical content of Reggae, and to this extent has always included "now" happenings. The "now" happenings referred to here, however, are the experience of the Dancehall. The sounds of the Dancehall are now viewed as Reggae was (at least in its country of birth) when it first made the scene, back in the sixties. It is a sound frowned upon by the Jamaican Establishment, whilst it has become the music of the "people".

Dancehall music which also had its beginnings in the sixties, gaining international currency in the seventies and becoming a dominant force in the eighties, is usually referred to as 'Hardcore Reggae', a term which causes Reggae purists to shudder. Hardcore it definitely is. For another audience I once classified it as "adult oriented Reggae". This clinical classification I thought appropriate at the time, because of the situation which obtained in Jamaica, where, in any given week, the top three records on the national charts would be Dancehall selections but listeners would never hear them played on the radio as they would usually be categorized as N.F.F.A. – 'Not fit for airplay'.

When this attempt at censorship failed to dampen interest, both the government-owned and the independent radio stations took the common decision not to include records with the N.F.F.A. classification, irrespective of sales generated, when compiling their weekly pop music charts. There are two points to note here. First, there was no contraction in record sales, and secondly, in some instances records designated N.F.F.A. and denied airplay in Jamaica, enjoyed airplay on the B.B.C. World Service, not to mention its domestic and British Forces Network.

The problem of the Dancehall phenomenon, as I understand it, and the problem it posed for those Directors of Programmes who took steps (and they are still in place) to censor the "sound", was that it is not deemed "living room music". That view may or may not be justified. It does not, however, seem to have had any effect on the appeal of the music which has risen above the provincial Jamaican shores. Its language – the reason for its N.F.F.A. downgrading – has been influencing North American rap music and British house music.

It is important to emphasize that while I am now committing to this Dictionary the words and expressions currently in use by the "originators" of the language, the language itself is not a static one but is constantly expanding, breaking new ground as it were. The reasons for this can be explained thus: in the specific area of Dancehall music, DJs who created and maintain this style of music do so in a very competitive environment, which demands of its exponents lyrical dexterity in order to survive. Reputations, and consequently the all-important recording contract, are secured by the DJ who is best able to chat lyrics from night till morning in the dancehall to hundreds of people who flock these usually small and restricting venues – usually a type of hall "put together" from bamboo, zinc, or any other discarded or inexpensive material, and designed with one objective in mind – those who enter must pay to do so!

Those who do, expect to be entertained. The DJ usually does this free of cost, or for a nominal fee, until he has established himself or has "a following" – fans who will visit a particular dance-hall if the DJ is appearing.

The DJ, per se, is not the creator of any actual music. What he in effect does is create a style of rapping, using every and anything – from his fans hygiene to their physical appearance and type of dress – as material for his performance. The promoters of the Dancehall packages customarily bill several DJs for one venue, to establish oneself as a "Don", or to maintain one's following and to grow in notoriety. Most performances approach the bizarre; others, sheer dramatic theatricality – all colourfully rich and innovative in language. This language is then set to the rhythm of a current Reggae hit or to a revived piece. Some DJs however, are now creating their own rhythms.

Until fairly recently, unlike the situation which obtained in the early stages of mainstream Reggae, Dancehall was an all-male turf, and as you will discover as you continue to flip these pages, despite its ghetto origins, the vocabulary developed by these ad-libbing DJs and nurtured by their fans – the conduit for this new language into the "mainstream" – is surprisingly right wing, almost reactionary. Even the tone of the language is definitely pro hot-blooded male heterosexual, almost to the point where it is regressively anti female. I hasten to add, the actual Dancehall environment, despite its language which is often uncomplimentary to the female, is a highly sexual one where the female is definitely the queen, and it is she who rules.

There is no disputing that the language of the Dancehall is primarily focused on actual sex. But this is no doubt because of the raw sexuality of the atmosphere of the Dancehall, highlighted by the various dance styles spawned in the Dancehall. The "Della Move", "Shoulder Move", "Horseman Skank", etc., are all dance styles which emphasize the general co-ordination of bodily movements around the central theme of a prescribed "move". However, there is an emphasis on groin movement running through all the dance styles emanating from the Dancehall, more obvious in 'moves' such as the "Water Pumpy", "Cool and Deadly", and the "Round de World". These are all styles which, through the execution of a series of well co-ordinated risqué movements take the mystery of bedroom debauchery right onto the dance floor.

In the early stages of the development of the Dancehall music (the early and mid sixties) the language associated with it was largely common-place. Words such as "gorgon", "ruler"; with expressions as "blouse 'n' skirt" – a swearing expression – were actually quite tepid. Nevertheless, the DJs of the era, King Stitch, U-Roy; and Big Youth; just to name a few, were not any less prolific than their successors.

Now, the language of the music is generally termed as "slackness lyrics". Interestingly, there is now more international interest in the sound, with a number of current DJs signing lucrative contracts with international recording and distribution companies, and the swelling ranks of DJs have grown to include a number of female performers.

In the ensuing pages, I have committed the words and expressions common to the Dancehall for the last few years. A number of these words, phrases, etc., have made and are continuing to make their way into pop culture, and English proper. Others may never make it, but will continue to enjoy extensive usage in the growing community of people constantly tuning in to the Dancehall sounds. Earlier I pointed out the crossover impact of the language. One example was when shortly after the Iraqui invasion of Kuwait, petrol became known as "Saddam" and was referred to as such for quite some time, a result of the skyrocketing effect the invasion had on the cost of petrol in Jamaica. Here an international event impacted on the music's vocabulary but it is also an example of that vocabulary's transitory nature, since when petrol price returned to its normal level, "Saddam" became obsolete.

This is an important fact to acknowledge at this time. The language constantly grows, adapting ew emphasis with each new DJ who, to make an impact, has to enter the existing fray with his own vocabulary and style of presentation. This also causes the established performers to come up with new material in order to maintain their validity. You will find, however, that within the context of the trend of the music, this dictionary will remain current, and will be of invaluable assistance to the newcomer to the music and to those who have always been with the "sound" but not quite hip to the meanings of some words and expressions that are associated with the music. And here I would like to add that the words and phrases addressed in this compilation run the gamut of emotions, from the amusing, ordinary, to the caustic.

INTRODUCTION

I have resisted earlier attempts by associates to have me compile this book and have it published as I fear that by so doing I will only further assist in the current sterilization of the music.

Dancehall music in its purest form, 'bubbling' with all the intensity, colour, and high drama of Kingston's urban ghettoes is at its best in its home environment. Attempts such as this to seek to shed light on this burgeoning music, for all the research etc., will always be superficial because of the inability to communicate the electricity, the atmosphere, in short, the vibes of the Dancehall, the home environment; whether this be in London, New York, Germany, Sweden, or in Jamaica.

The Dancehall and the music it gave birth to, is an experience which spawned its own food, drink, fashion and, case in point, language. The original music itself draws heavily on the colourful Jamaican experience, using a vocabulary that is totally visually descriptive.

Figuring prominently in the music's vocabulary are the more notorious of Jamaican ghettoes;

references to the island's two major political parties, and their strongholds; and the choicest of 'cusswords'. The harmonious combining of these and other experiences has evolved into the sheer theatrical drama of Dancehall music. It is intended that this compendium will offer more than a summary interest to the reader but will create an experience akin to the reality.

And while the language paints and illustrates the music, and graphically so, earning itself the label 'slackness' – much to the dismay of Reggae purists, notably columnists – interest in the music, its relatively obscure lyrical content notwithstanding, has not been diminishing as has been predicted. In fact we can say that in spite of the relatively foreign language in which Dancehall is sung, recorded, etc., interest in the music has skyrocketed internationally.

'Trend?' I think not. 'Phase?' Nope!

Labels such as these are, at best, superficial attempts to explain away the Dancehall phenomenon in pretty much the same way that attempts were made to curtail the phenomenon of Reggae before Bob Marley accorded it respectability. These labels ignore the development and history of what is now the phenomena booming from sets, Nigga Boxes, and being worked on dancefloors in Jamaica, the USA, Britain, Germany, Italy, France, Poland and /or Ibizia.

In an interesting and informed programme on the subject of Dancehall carried by the BBC in May of 1991, the question was posed: Was Jamaica now turning its back on **Roots Reggae** (my emphasis) à la Bob Marley? The interviewee, Neville Garrick, friend of the late Bob Marley and who now directs the Bob Marley Museum in Kingston, Jamaica, replied, 'No'. And indeed 'no' it is. Dancehall music may have gained international prominence within the last two years or so, but it was there right from the very birth of Reggae, in a class titled then and now as Ragamuffin. While reggae went on to earn respectability and its place on international play-lists, the Dancehall 'Ragamuffin' sound took hold in the ghettoes of Jamaica.

The music is admittedly still largely identifiable only with ghetto circumstances, albeit on an international scale. And those who radically label it 'trend' – and a passing one too – rush to point out (as a means of bolstering their position) that the music is yet to storm into international charts and yet to be of significance by way of longevity. But this is in reality an expression of the ignorance of the music itself.

The current popularity of the music was not achieved through the slick and professional promotion accorded mainstream music. Dancehall made its way from the ghettoes of Kingston via the underground – chanting 'slackness', debasing our womenfolk, and appealing to our baser instincts all the way. Its pathway consisted largely of 'specialist record shops' and the creative machinations of a few individuals, with practically little or no airplay – the surest way of crossing-over and the surest conventional method of attracting attention – outside of 'specialist stations', or programmes. The exception here was John Peal of BBC Radio 1 – a local, that is to say, a British-based radio station that consistently plays both Reggae and Dancehall.

Mainstream radio largely ignores Dancehall Reggae: a number of reasons being advanced include: programme directors not 'liking' the sound or 'slackness' content; the violence; etc., and etc. But the music itself is no longer that of the underground crowd. (Who wants to keep a good thing to themselves?) It has now established itself as a floor-filler on the mainstream scene. This has led to some mainstream dance acts seeking to engender a new style incorporating Dancehall into... you name it, it's being attempted. And, herein lies the greatest fad potential.

Of 'slackness': In the mid 1980s, at about the time when the musical world was caught up in Bob Marley nostalgia following on his death, Winston Foster, an orphan who had spent his growing years at Eventide Home, a home primarily for the aged, infirm and indigent, situated smack in the middle of many of Kingston's ghettoes, rose to DJ prominence and very soon after was hailed as DJ King. Bob Marley, the King of Reggae was dead, a new king was crowned, albeit not of 'Reggae' but of Reggae's underside.

Winston Foster, an orphaned albino though in his teens, and truly a physically unattractive young man, took the stage name 'Yellowman' (an acknowledgement of his being an albino, a physical state which automatically stigmatized him and shunted him to the edge of society as an abnormal freak) and became, paradoxically, the darling of the new generation of Reggae lovers, using lyrics that tore everything apart.

He spared nothing. Himself, homosexuality, the various ethnic groups of Jamaica, the prevailing social order, and the social practices and habits of his audience then – the underprivileged underclass – were all taken to task in the 'raw-chaw' language of the environment. As his popularity increased and his lyrics (not fit for airplay) began being recited by four and five-year-olds, the Jamaican media took an active interest in his lyrics, branded as indecently offensive, and degrading to women.

Yellowman achieved cult-like status, and curiously enough, his popularity soared, particularly among women

And what is 'slackness'? As performed by

Yellowman and as is being performed today by practitioners of the art, it is the ability to unabashedly call a spade, a spade – the word sex may be more pleasant to the ear, but 'fuck' is what, by and large, is meant, so this is the word used, or the current substitute common to the vocabulary and experience of Dancehall 'massives'.

Of 'culture': Of the other style of DJing practised by Dancehall DJs, 'Culture' is the name given to this vein. The 'cultural' DJ deals with 'livity' and 'up-fullness' – he avoids the usage of 'slackness' lyrics and basically sees himself as part of the musical process promoting social consciousness, awareness, and change.

Basically, the 'slackness DJ' sees himself as a social commentator. On the other hand, the 'cultural DJ' operates as a social activist – a vehicle for change. Of the two it is the latter – the 'cultural DJ' – who, artistically, identifies with the lyrical legacy of Bob Marley (that is, within the dancehall vein).

Since Yellowman first unleashed 'slackness' (to a receptive public), several Dancehall DJs have emerged from out of the musical woodwork riding the 'slackness' rhythm all the way to the bank. With this new and growing trend have come the new 'styles' of DJing. Not all the new crop of DJs 'check fi de slackness' but the awareness that 'a slackness time now' has led to an inventiveness, both among those who DJ in praise of 'slackness' and those 'inclined' to promote 'culcha', which has only enriched the dancehall 'stylee'. The tendency by the commentator to label all Dancehall 'style' as 'ragga', is off mark.

'Ragga', or Ragamuffin – the actual parent of 'Ragga' which these same commentators wrongly claim to be a sort of unwanted, black sheep if you like, offspring of Reggae – is just one of many prevailing styles. And as the word ragamuffin indicates, this 'style' is hardcore dancehall stuff, lyrically. The heavy dub – instrumental, characterized by a heavy bass – will be found in all styles. And here I point out, style is used to indicate:

(a) personal delivery
(b) general vein, as in: dub-wise, ragamuffin, rub-a-dub, lovers-rock, or slackness.

Within the Dancehall DJ fraternity it is those with a distinctive individual style – a consistent wheeze; a banshee like wail; a gravelly sound; stuttering; chanting; or the ability to rhyme, all backed with theatricality – who author and enjoy 'don-like' status.

And, whichever vein a performance DJ makes his own, the lyrical content of Dancehall music has been, and remains largely anecdotal. Where it is alleged that DJs advocate violence, this is arguable as what is usually alluded to is defensive violence. The exception is violence as an act of aggression against male and female homosexuals. And this prejudice, while not excusable, on the face of it, could be said to be a Jamaican trait, amplified by the ghetto circumstances which provides the inspiration for the lyrics to the music.

As stated earlier: Reggae music is largely available from "specialist" shops. This is especially true of Europe, but in North America this is not the prevailing mode – a situation which tends to contribute to the marginalization of the music. However, where there is a recognition of the sales potential, Reggae charts are used to quantify sales. Interestingly, where these charts obtain (they do on both sides of the Atlantic) it is the Dancehall strain of Reggae which is in the ascendancy, particularly the 'slackness' style. That Shabba Ranks was signed to CBS – the biggest reggae signing in recent history – is an acknowledgement of the status of Dancehall reggae – long an established part of the Jamaican dance scene. The recent inroads it has been making on the international scene says it's more than 'the flavour of the month'.

But more on the music: Reggae has been described thus – a type of popular music from the West Indies with a strong, continually repeated beat; the music from the Caribbean island of Jamaica made popular by Bob Marley, characterized by its heavy, often repeated bass.

The Collins Dictionary gives this definition: Reggae – a type of West Indian popular music having four beats to the bar, the upbeat being strongly accentuated.

All these definitions of the word Reggae, taken from these different sources stress the 'repeated' bass line. Dancehall style has not yet earned a place in world dictionaries but it would be interesting to see what definition it would be accorded. Unlike Reggae, Dancehall style is not necessarily identified by its heavy repeated bass line. In fact, quite often, the bass line does not exist at all, and the 'accent' is away from the bass and on the artiste. It is the 'style' the artistes perfect which largely accounts for Dancehall's popularity. Lyrics and bass follow.

And, when it comes to the rhythm (bass) the tendency has been to move away from the 'accented' standard Reggae bass line to a more up-tempo type rhythm a sort of electro exploration – with liberal samplings from soul and/or disco material. The end result is that while Reggae's bass line is its identity card, Dancehall, while it incorporates the bass line, has moved away from within the structures of the established rhythm to embrace a wider expression. In short, the bass line is no longer king.

This up-tempo style rhythm, with its electro-exploration and sampling, it should be noted, often follows a pace that is dictated by the particular DJ's style.

The DJ Tiger with his hoarse throaty roar, Ninja Man with his stammering (stuttering) style; the wailing Sweetie Irie, are a few examples of the main characteristics of Dancehall music: the music (rhythm) is usually composed after the lyrics, to accommodate the DJ's style. The most common method, however, of putting together Dancehall music, at least by the majority of new-comers and a few 'ranking' DJs is to adapt an existing rhythm to facilitate the DJ's style. Often, adapted versions of established rhythms show no real, or noticeable rearrangement. And, when a rhythm or a whole record achieves Dancehall prominence, whether its origins are in soul, disco, Dancehall etc., the adapted versions will number in their tens of tens.

Rhythms, and/or records are not the only areas of Dancehall where large scale adaptation occurs or is attempted. For every successful DJ with his own 'inimitable' style, there are several aspirants to be found imitating him. This trend is not only confined to Jamaica but is also to be found in cities such as Toronto, Miami, New York and London.

But of particular relevance to this compilation is the growing awareness of, and the effect Dancehall is having on, the wider music and new-music world. Not only has there been a growing interest, internationally, in Dancehall reggae, but there has been a corresponding awareness of, and active interest in its sub-culture and language. As the streets and corners of most musical cities, particularly those with large ghettoes, underground culture, faddish population, continue to blast Dancehall music from motor vehicles and sets, the language of these specific populations has been changing: 'The new talk' comes straight out of the Dancehall. To be sure, many using the language do so without fully grasping the essence of the spoken word – as one German acquaintance of mine, after attending a Reggae Dancehall 'Shakedown' in Berlin went about for days reciting a line he'd picked up from one of the many performing DJs. The line 'she just a kin out her saul' which in as approximate a translation as is attainable, means: 'she's exposing her vagina,' was not at all understood by my German acquaintance, but because 'it sounded cool', and was used by a currently 'stinging' DJ he thought it very hip to be using it. He had, however, the accent and emphasis down to a tee. Needless to say I was, and still am amused whenever I think of my acquaintance happily humming: 'she jus a kin out'.

In the opening paragraph of this introduction I stated that I had reservations about contributing, however unwittingly, to the sterilization of Dancehall music. Like Calypso, which originated in the Caribbean isles of Trinidad and Tobago, the lyrical component cannot be separated from the sound any more than in the case of Dancehall. The tendency to classify Dancehall as 'slackness' is ill-informed. 'Slackness' is but one of many Dancehall styles.

So, why this dictionary? With the language of the Dancehall becoming more widely spoken by Dancehall enthusiasts, it is experiences such as those with my German acquaintance referred to earlier, plus my having viewed an interview given by a group of young musicians (a pop group) in which they laid claim to being originators of a number of Dancehall words, which spurred me to compile this book.

I fervently hope that in picking it up you will find it illuminating, entertaining and will have a much deeper insight into the music and the culture it sprang from.

CHESTER FRANCIS-JACKSON

A Basic Guide to Understanding the Jamaican Language

The Jamaican language is largely a derivative of the Spanish, English and African influences on the island through its colonial heritage. English, though, is the officially recognized tongue of the island, but it is the homegrown derivative which is used by the majority of the population, moreso, in the island's ghettoes – the home of Dancehall music. However, of the three influences that have been identified, the English language is the dominating force, and it is this language that the homegrown language most closely resembles.

There are a number of distinguishing features of the home-grown language which set it apart; three of which are common to Reggae and Dancehall music as it's contribution which helps to add colour to both sounds.

They are set out below:

1. The 'th' sound of English, when transliterated give a 'd' sound.
   Example: This = Dis.

2. Unlike the Russian alphabet where the 'h' does not exist, it does in the Jamaican alphabet but is often pronounced, as in Cockney, before vowels, but not where you'd expect to hear it in Standard English.

Example: Me put me 'an hinto de 'at wata.

'an = hand
'at = hot
hinto = into.

3. The tendency overall is to 'round up one's mouth' when one speaks resulting in 'a's being pronounced 'o' etc., and vice versa.

Examples:

man = mon
borrow = barra
hardly = ordly.

Of course, there are exceptions to the stated principles; and it should be emphasized that not all Dancehall DJs record in Jamaican. Some use English.

Special Note

Obviously, this is not your conventional Dictionary. However, it will seek to maintain, as far is practicable, the conventional approach of listing entries in alphabetical order.

The words used, or some of them, may appear foreign. Where the words listed are not obviously English, their origins will be identified. The identification code is set below:

Ja. = Jamaican
Spn. = Spanish
Af. = African

Example: **Bandoolu** *(Ja)* a trickster.

KEYS

Figures are used to indicate the number of interpretations. The letter *u.* indicates Dancehall usage, often followed by an appropriate English translation.

The complete key is

Af.	–	African
Ja	–	Jamaican
Spn.	–	Spanish
F. or M.	–	Gender
U.	–	Usage
1.2	–	List of interpretations
Derog.	–	Derogatory
Vul.	–	Vulgar
Off.	–	Offensive

N.B. The language is largely situational and 'flexes' to the occasion. To this end syntactical classifications such as nouns, adverbs, etc., are not entered into the key.

THE GENESIS

In 1987 writer Chester Francis-Jackson was commissioned by *Profile* magazine to do a feature on the then burgeoning Dancehall music and the sub-culture it sprang from. As a result of this research, *Profile* published an article in November of the same year entitled "Dancehall Vocabulary". The Dancehall dictionary is as a direct outgrowth of this commission. The original article is included here with the kind permission of the publishers of *Profile* magazine.

Dancehall Vocabulary

Are you a Dancehall fan? Are you familiar with the Dancehall language? Maybe you have a child in high school and you often overhear him speaking in a somewhat foreign tongue – that is; it's not Patois, English, or anything you have heard before for that matter. Does it make you feel older? It shouldn't. Dancehall talk is seldom spoken anywhere but at the Dancehall; and more often than not is only understood by the Dancehall goer.

I have discovered that the Dancehall language is usually done on the spur of the moment usually when there is a line-up of DJs performing and they, in trying to outdo the other in adlibbing, concoct new phrases and words. It is important to note that the current language or Dancehall terminologies change as quickly as we have a new DJ.

In compiling this list of words and phrases for your better understanding of your 'youth' you will find the relatively common place 'yow' a form of greeting, and the crude 'punani' translated 'vagina'.

But not to worry: if you know that 'hol a fresh' means taking a shower and that 'a my ting' means, 'it's my girl', you are not as dated as you think.

One thing that is clear though is that some of these words and phrases are totally incomprehensible and really mean nothing unless you are the 'originator'.

For instance, a current phrase 'no fren yu mate' a line in a hit DJ style, Dancehall dub, has no clear meaning to the many women who go wild when they hear the chant, and even though it is spreading from 'Metro' (where I first heard it) to other Dancehalls, the effect is the same.

So OK – here is a list of words and phrases you might hear from a neighbour, or your youth, or even at the workplace.

Back off: cool it/take it easy
Be nice: be nice
Bubble: to dance
Bubbler: dancer
Bus shot/lick shot: fire gun
Cease 'n' settle: to stop and be cool
Chill: being cool
Chilling out: staying put
Di Don: respected one
Di I a flash: I am leaving
Drop a fa shape: not looking good
Dub: heavy music (instrumental) or a type of dance

Flash it: to allow (usually music)

Forward: to repeat

Glimity Glamity: virginal state

Hol yu corner: staying put

"John Crow yu waa flap a wing": Girl would you like to dance?

Let off: to give something

Maas yuh face: hide your face

Peel mi something: beg you something (money)

Posse: friends or group

Request to: dedicated to

Settle: be cool

She a clean rifle: she indulges in oral sex

Smoke: ganja

Tan pon it long: staying power (sexual)

Trash: dressed

Tranquillo: to be cool

Oil: semen

THE OFFICIAL DANCEHALL DICTIONARY

A **1.** I **2.** used with a verb to form the continuous tense: *u.* weh yuh **a** go?/*where are you going?*

Aataclaps a calamity: *u.* what a aataclaps.

After-Birth a rude remark embodying total contempt to whomever it is directed.

Agony rough sex: *u.* gi' me de agony.

Ali-button to be somebody's fool.

Alms'ouse negative in behaviour or attitude.

Artist con artist: *u.* min' de artist fool yuh/*do not allow yourself to be conned.*

EXPRESSIONS

All fruits ripe all women are potentially sex partners.

A we run things we are in charge here.

A would a deh wid yuh I am attracted to you and would like to sleep with you.

texttext 2

B-bwoy an abbreviation of Batty Boy: *u.* we nuh check fi nuh b-bwoy/*we do not care for homosexuals.*

Babylon 1. a disrespectful term for police officer: *u.* Babylon bway 2. an oppressive situation: *u.* dis yah a Babylon/*this is hell.*

Back-weh move away, back off, usually a command to step back: *u.* back-weh, bwoy.

Back-yard buttocks: *u.* 'ar backyard 'eavy/*she has a well padded behind.*

Backitive collateral; cash; influential friend: *u.* me 'ave backitive.

Backsiding a thorough and severe thrashing: *u.* gi' de yout' a backsiding.

Bad-mind envious; wishing someone ill: *u.* bad-minded person.

Bad-wud swear word; 'cussword'.

Bade *(Ja.)* to make a killing: *u.* 'im horse win an' 'im bade.

Baggy female underwear, panty.

Baldhead non-rastafarians; of unrighteous behaviour.

Bammy flat type of bread made from cassava.

Bandoolu *(Ja.)* to use trickery; trickster: *u.* to bandoolu someone.

Bang-a-rang noisy disturbance; commotion, confusion.

Banton to affect a superior attitude.

Barrows a monetary loan; anything borrowed: *u.* beg yuh a barrows.

Base **1.** one's home **2.** to touch base/to be in contact.

Bat-bat the buttocks; bottom.

Bath a bath specially prepared with herbs by an 'obeah man' to ward off evil; a special trip to the beach to keep off ill-luck.

Batta-Foot an ordinary person: *u.* batta-foot gal.

Battery 1. two or more men having sexual intercourse with one female: *u.* dem battery de gal. **2.** a lone male using performance enhancing substance during intercourse.

Batty buttocks.

Batty-man *(vul.)* a homosexual: *u.* we nuh deal wid batty-man.

Batty-rider a skirt or pair of shorts which exposes more of the buttocks than it conceals.

Bawl-out anything dramatically eye catching: *u.* de car a bawl-out, rasta.

Bax the act of slapping someone in the face: *u.* A wi' bax yuh, yuh know.

Bax-bout *(derog.)* to drift aimlessly: *u.* bax-bout bwoy.

Beef a woman: *u.* a criss beef; de beef ripe, star/*she's a lovely woman*.

Belly 1. the stomach or any part of the abdomen **2.** state of pregnancy: *u.* dash-wey belly/*to have an abortion*. (See also **Running Belly**).

Bex vexed, angry, annoyed.

Bhutto of coarse behaviour; a person lacking in sophistication.

Big-bwoy the lovable idiot of Jamaican folklore; village idiot.

Big-time major; foremost; very good: *u.* she a big-time dancer.

Bingo-bag full-sized underwear.

Blar to show off: *u.* A blar she a blar/*she's showing off.*

Blender a character with the penchant for causing or creating conflict: *u.* me know yuh a ol' blender.

Bless (to bless someone) abuse verbally: *u.* if she badda yuh, bless har.

Blood-fire a denunciation: *u.* blood-fire fi all batty-bwoy.

Bly an opportunity; chance: *u.* a need a bly.

Bombo-red vagina.

Boo an idiot: *u.* de bwoy a boo.

Boogu-yagga *(Ja.)* **1.** an unattractive person. **2.** of coarse or common behaviour.

Boops sugar daddy (see **Brinks**): *u.* de man is har boops.

Booster sexual stimulant, aphrodisiac.

Boots condoms: *u.* man mus' always ride wid 'im boots.

Bounce to have intercourse: *u.* me bounce de gal last night.

Bow (to bow) to indulge in oral sex.

Bow-cat a man who indulges in fellatio.

Bram-bram a celebratory expression, imitating the sound of gun-fire.

Brawta extras; surplus: *u.* beg yuh a brawta/*may I have some extras.*

Breads money: *u.* let-off some breads/*can you spare some change?*

Breed 1. to be pregnant: *u.* de gal a breed/*she's pregnant.* 2. to breathe.

Bright daring; precocious: *u.* de likkle pickney bright, yuh see.

Bringle to show extreme annoyance, displeasure: *u.* de man cause I to bringle, rasta.

Brinks a sugar daddy.

Broad massive; big; influential: *u.* de man broad, star/*he is influential.*

Brought-upsy up-bringing: *u.* yuh nuh 'ave no brought-upsy.

Browning light-complexioned girl, not quite a mulatto: *u.* me love mi browning bad.

Bruk 1. being without cash: *u.* I man bruk, star **2.** an orgasm: *u.* A bruk some water, star.

Bruk-out to let loose, to become wild or promiscuous.

Bubble 1. type of dance rotating the pelvic area. **2.** to be on top of the world.

Buck 1. to meet with someone: *u.* Buck yuh up later/*see you later.* **2.** to strike with the forehead, as a goat.

Buddy the penis.

Bumm-shot mega bad; happening: *u.* de music a bumm-shot.

Bumper the behind: *u.* woman, me love yu bumper/*I love your rear end.*

Bun 1. burn **2.** act of infidelity (usually of a woman, without her partner's knowledge): *u.* she a gi' 'im bun.

Bus' water ejaculate

Bus-out 1. to make it big, to enjoy success. **2.** to reveal, let the cat out of the bag.

Bush well groomed: *u.* de chick well bush.

Butter any feat requiring no effort; easily done: *u.* a butter dat.

EXPRESSIONS

Back 'n' belly rat the gossiper who carries tales to and fro.

Back-yuh fist male masturbation.

Big bout yah famous, influential.

Big up yuh chest to assume an air of importance.

Big up yuhself enjoy your status, you've earned it.

Body-come-down to lose weight dramatically; to look haggard; to lose one's sex appeal.

Bruk-mi-ducks one's very first experience, usually sexually (reference to moving off the mark – ducks – in cricket).

Ca'k having a capacity crowd: *u.* de dance ca'k.

Cabba-cabba *(Ja. vul.)* of low quality; not well groomed.

Callie a potent form of ganja distinguished by its seedlessness and fluffy buds.

Cargo heavy gold chains with or without huge adorning medallions.

Carry-feelings to bear a grudge: *u.* de bwoy a carry feelings fi me.

Cawn (corn) **1.** money **2.** bullets: *u.* me bus' two cawn.

Cemetry name given (usually shouted at) women known or suspected of having had an abortion: *u.* ol' cemetry.

Chaka-chaka a general state of untidiness: *u.* yuh dress chaka-chaka.

Charge high; stoned; euphoric state induced by drugs, etc.

Chatty-chatty the act of speaking too much; a chatter-box.

Check to pay someone a visit: *u.* to check mi brethren.

Check-fah/fi to be fond of: *u.* me check fi da' gal deh.

Check-out to observe keenly: *u.* to check-out de scene.

Cherry 1. virginity: *u.* to pick her cherry/ *deflowering a virgin* 2. feeling mellow: *u.* to feel cherry.

Chill to be cool: *u.* jus' chill/*be cool; don't get excited.*

Chillum the water pipe used by many for the smoking of ganja, especially by those who smoke it as a part of a religious rite.

Chiney-brush sexual performance enhancer: *u.* to chiney-brush de gal.

Chopper sub-machine gun.

Chuck to behave as a toughie; to shove someone.

Chuckie local toughie.

Clarkes name-brand footwear popular among Dancehall enthusiasts.

Clyde cloy: *u.* de honey clyde me/*the honey is cloying.*

Coca-cola shape the perfectly proportioned female.

Cock-up 1. of or relating to a sexual position 2. to sit in a vulgar manner.

Cockaty to affect airs: *u.* de gal a gwaan too cockaty/*she is much too affected.*

Cocksman a man with a reputation of being a good lover.

Coil a substantial amount of cash: *u.* to 'ol a coil.

Come-aroun' an ordinary individual who usualy hangs around where he/she is not welcome but is tolerated.

Concorde the Jamaican hundred-dollar bill, so named because of the relative ease with which it 'disappears': *u.* let off a concorde.

Consignment the term used to describe cheating, usually shouted at a person out with a date who is known to be seeing someone else: *u.* de gal deh pon consignment.

Cool-runnings a greeting: *u.* cool runnings, man/*everything is O.K.*

Coot *(off.)* idiot: *u.* yuh nuh see seh yuh a coot.

Copasetic *(Ja.)* all is well: *u.* everything copasetic.

Count to count someone; to hold the person in high esteem.

Crabbit *(Ja.)* **1.** good: *u.* a crabbit piece of music **2.** coarse individual: *u.* yuh too crabbit.

Craven greedy, gluttonous: *u.* yuh too craven/ *you're a glutton.*

Crebs *(off.)* low life.

Crib the home: *u.* me a go a mi crib.

Criss anything new or attractive: *u.* de outfit criss; de gal criss.

Criss-biscuit well-dressed person; very attractive.

Curry-favour to kiss ass: *u.* de bwoy too curry-favour.

Cut-eye to stare malevolently then turn away with eyes closed: *u.* nuh cut yuh eye after me.

EXPRESSIONS

Carry-go-bring-come tale bearing.

Cease 'n' settle be cool; usually a dancehall command issued by the performing DJ to the mixing DJ.

Clean-de-rifle to perform oral sex: *u.* dem gal deh clean-rifle.

Cry-champagne to express one's emotions dramatically.

Da'k backward; illiterate, not sophisticated: *u.* 'im da'k yuh see/*he's very stupid, dumb.*

Dads a community or corner leade

Damage-goods of a woman who has lost her virtue: *u.* me no wan' nuh damage-goods.

Dash weh belly to commit an abortion: *u.* dem gal deh dash weh belly.

Dawg to be disrespectful to: *u.* to dawg someone.

Dawta young woman: *u.* dawta, yuh a seh one/*girl, you're looking good.*

Dead-stock not happening; a non-event: *u.* dead-stock business.

Deadas of meat: *u.* mi nuh check fi deadas/*I don't eat meat.*

Degeh-degeh used to emphasise a small amount or one: *u.* a de one degeh-degeh frock she 'av.

Deh 1. be, is, are: *u.* nobaddy no deh ya/*nobody is here* **2.** there.

Deh deh be there: *u.* a who deh deh?/*who is there?*

Deh wid to be intimate: *u.* a woulda deh wid yuh (a crude but acceptable proposal of intimacy).

Dem-deh those

Dem ya these

Des desperation: *u.* star, I man des/*I am in a state of desperation.*

Dibby-dibby *(Ja. derog.)* low life: *u.* dibby-dibby bwoy.

Digital state of the art; modern.

Ding to telephone someone: *u.* a wi' gi' yuh a ding.

Dippy a deportee: *u.* a British dippy/*a deportee from Britain.*

Diss to show disrespect: *u.* a diss you a diss me?/*are you showing me disrespect?*

Don title of respect, not necessarily of a criminal.

Don't test intended to imply one's superiority; a statement of one-upmanship: *u.* nuh bwoy don't test.

Don-dada father of dons; the highest in the hierarchy of 'dons'.

Don-gorgan an enforcer.

Donna general name for all look-able females.

Donovan *(derog.)* a pretender to the role and title of 'Don'.

Drape the act of grabbing someone in the waist and hoisting him onto his toes: *u.* drape de bwoy.

Drapers suspenders, braces.

Draw-down to make an approach; initial contact: *u.* to drawn-down pon a ting/*to make a sexual advance.*

Dread rastafarian.

Dress-back a command to step back a few paces.

Drop out dying suddenly or unexpectedly, especially under tragic circumstances: *u.* John drop out las' week, star.

Drop pan an illegal numbers game.

Drop wud to make indirect comments about someone who is usually close enough to hear them.

Drop-it to affect a street attitude in clothes, mannerisms, walk, and speech etc., those who have perfected this style are said to 'drop-it': *u.* de yout' a drop it.

Dropsy illness relating to anyone who suffers or is prone to falling asleep almost anywhere at anytime: *u.* de bwoy 'ave dropsy.

Druggist dancehall buzzword, includes but does not necessarily mean illegal drug traffickers or users: *u.* druggist, weh yuh a seh?

Dry malice to pointedly ignore someone by using a third party to communicate, even when within hearing of each other.

Dry-eye barefaced; daring: *u.* a dry-eye person.

Dub **1.** heavy instrumental **2.** type of dance characterised by slow pelvic crunching movements **3.** to hit upon someone.

Dugu-dugu sexual intercourse.

Dun done; finished: *u.* me dun wid it/*I'm finished with it.*

Dung down: *u.* it dung deh.

Dungle ordinary, of no account: *u.* yuh a no body, yuh a dungle.

Dunsie money.

Duppy 1. a ghost 2. an unattractive person.

Duppy-conqueror fearless person.

Dus' to attack, even kill someone: *u.* to dus' de bwoy dem.

Dutchie cast iron pot used for frying, cooking, etc., a dutch-pot.

Dutty dirty: *u.* dutty bwoy, go 'bout yuh business.

EXPRESSIONS

Dancehall teh-teh dancehall enthusiast.

Dis de program to show disregard, disrespect.

Drop-off-a-style to lose one's sexiness, figure, etc.

Ease-off keep your distance: *u.* de man fi ease-off, star.

Engka *(derog.)* to hang around with the intentions of mooching: *u.* yuh too engka.

Even-up *(derog.)* presumptuousness; assuming the liberties of friendship before they are extended: *u.* yuh too even-up.

Everyt'ing is everyt'ing everything is O.K.

Exercise-me a request to dance: *u.* yow champion, yuh wan' exercise me.

Extra a show-off; being etc.: *u.* de gal too extra/*she likes to flaunt herself.*

EXPRESSIONS

Eat-unda-table of man who indulges in oral sex.

F

Faas to be inquisitive: *u.* yuh love faas eena people business.

Facialist *(Ja.)* a woman who indulges in oral sex.

Family-ram *(derog.)* incestous males; any male who indulges in any incestuous relationship or sleeps with more than one female from the same family.

Fanciness jewellery, expensive clothing, etc.

Fancy-girl material girl (à la Madonna).

Fava to resemble, to look like: *u.* me fava eedi-at?/*do I look like a fool?*

Ferculate *(Ja.)* light cuss word: *u.* don't fercu-late/*don't play around.*

Festival a type of fried roll prepared from flour, cornmeal and sugar.

Filicity facility: **u.** no filicity fi dat.

Fire-bun an expression of denunciation which originated from the rastafarian sect: *u.* fire-bun fi all pork eaters!

Flash-it (usually of music) to start up or allow to continue.

Flex hot dancehall buzzword (due mainly to a hit by Jamaican DJ, Cobra, titled **Flex... time to have sex**) meaning ready for sex.

Fluxy immature; having loose body fat; (of people, fruits): *u.* fluxy bwoy.

Force-ripe *(derog.)* precociousness: *u.* yuh too force-ripe.

Force-up *(derog.)* a social climber: *u.* she too force-up.

Foreign-mind of Jamaicans with a foreign (usually North American) attitude characterized by speech, dress etc.

French cut fancy underwear.

Fresh-vegetable a young man being dated by an older woman.

Frig-up *(vul.)* to screw up: *u.* de man frig-up de program.

Frighten easily impressed; nouveau riche: *u.* she too frighten.

Fryers unimportant person; a small timer; a sidekick: *u.* go weh, yuh a fryers.

EXPRESSIONS

Fatty bum-bum a term of affection for the attractively fat woman.

Feel-bad being ill: *u.* a feel bad, yuh see/*I'm not feeling well, at all.*

Fling-it-up wild abandon (of dancing or inter-course) *u.* she can fling it up.

Ganja local name for marijuana.

Ginnal *(Ja.)* a trickster; con-man: *u.* 'im a big time ginnal.

Girlie-girlie casanova type; philanderer: *u.* de bwoy girlie-girlie.

Gizzada tart filled with coconut and sugar.

Gladys *(derog.)* a person unaccustomed to wealth who acquires some or is exposed to that of others, and falls in awe to the point of gushing.

Glammity a woman's vaginal prowess or ability: *u.* gi me de glammity.

Goody-goody a 'Miss goody two-shoes'.

Gorgan a toughie; roughneck: *u.* de man is a gorgan.

Gravalicious *(Ja.)* greedy; grasping attitude or behaviour, avaricious.

Green unpleasant body odor: *u.* yuh smell green.

Grine to copulate, *also* grind.

Gritty-ball *(Ja.)* the clitoris; the female pleasure centre: *u.* to touch the gritty-ball/*to give the ultimate pleasure*.

Grizzle the clitoris.

Grudgeful malicious envy: *u.* de people dem too grudgeful.

Gumption (see **Glammity**).

Gun-salute the practice of firing weapons at dancehall venues as a sign of respect, endorsement to one's favourite artiste.

Guzzu *(Ja.)* **1.** ill fortune **2.** obeah: *u.* dem set guzzu pon me.

Gwa'an go on, continue: *u.* gwa'an an yuh wi fin' out/*Continue what you are doing and you will suffer the consequences.*

Gwey go away: *u.* gwey, bwoy!/*Get away from me!*

EXPRESSIONS

Gal a tek life a woman who is a head turner; a very attractive or well-dressed woman.

Gun eena baggy a female suffering from a veneral infection, usually gonorrhea: *u.* de gal a carry gun eena ar baggy.

Gwaan wid it take it all the way (usually music): *u.* gwaan wid it, DJ.

Hairy-bank the vagina. A man who is generous to his girlfriend by giving gifts of jewellery, cash, etc. is said to be making deposits at hairy-bank.

(H)aity-taity affecting an air of grandness, having one's nose in the air.

(H)arbour-shark a greedy, grasping individual: *u.* mek de 'ol harbour-shark, gwaan.

(H)art-attack an expression used to sum up one's feeling after seeing anything theatrically or dramatically eye-catching: *u.* gal, yuh gi' me (h)art-attack.

(H)eavy 1. influential 2. being armed: *u.* de brethren well heavy.

H)eavy-man 1. a man of influence; influential person 2. an armed man.

(H)erb the general name for marijuana.

(H)ol' it dung avoid getting excited; play it cool: *u.* big man, hol' it dung, nuh.

(H)ol' tight be cool; stay cool: *u.* hol' tight, mi brethren.

(H)ol-yuh-corner to remain on one's turf: *u.* man fi hol 'im corner/*don't invade my space.*

(H)ome-bwoy one's country man.

(H)ood penis.

Hortical (also artical) esteem, rank, etc: **u.** hortical don.

(H)ot-number a sexy female: *u.* de gal Sharon deh a hot number.

EXPRESSIONS

Haul 'n' pull-up usually a command by a performing DJ to his 'selector' to stop or effect a pause in the rhythm being played.

Hol' a fresh go take a shower: *u.* bwoy, go hol' a fresh.

Iah friend; term of comradeship: *u.* wha' a gwaan, iah.

Idle jubbie youths with no obvious means of support or employment.

Idren brethren; friend: *u.* 'im a mi bona fide idren.

Ilaloo the name given to the vegetable calaloo by the rastafarians.

Indica a grade of marijuana known by its shorter leaves.

Irie (often used as a greeting) good, great; at Reggae sessions when the performer asks – 'how yuh feelin?', *irie* as a response means super.

Irish potato the term given to the young men dated by older women, a 'kept' young man.

Ishen marijuana of a potent form grown in the hilly areas; money.

Ital natural and organic when relating to food; salt-free; when the subject is sex the interpretation is condom-free: *u.* ital food; ital sex.

Italist a naturalist.

J.A. Jamaica

Jacket a man who unknowingly accepts the social responsibility of fatherhood for a child not thought to be his genetic off-spring: *u.* a fi 'im jacket that.

Jagga-bite of the lowest class and behaviour: *u.* me nuh mix wid jagga-bite.

Jah rastafari name for God; term of brotherly love.

Jah-know an oath; expression uttered to add credence to a claim or a statement: *u.* Jah-know me check fi de sistren/*I really like the young lady.*

Jah-Rastafari God, the most high.

Jam capacity crowd: *u.* de dance last nite did jam, iah; (to jam) to have a good time; staying put.

Jamdung Jamaica

Jammin dancing and having a good time.

Jim-screechy sneaky, underhand: *u.* wha' kin' a jim-screechy business dat?

Jing-bang of the lower classes; inappropriate behaviour: *u.* yuh nuh see 'im a jing-bang.

Jook *(Ja.)* to stick, as with a pin: *u.* jook 'im wid it.

Jubbie *(Ja.)* a young friend, a girlfriend.

Judgement strife, serious consequences of an action: *u.* judgement on yah tonight if 'im see yuh.

Jugglin 1. type of dance 2. hustling.

Juice 1. sperm: *u.* to bruck a juice 2. alcohol: *u.* to drink up some juice.

Junjo mildew; fungus; also used as a 'put-down' when directed at a person: *u.* gwey, yuh ol' junjo, yuh.

EXPRESSIONS

John-crow, yuh waan flap a wing term used to ask someone to dance: *u.* gal, yuh waan flap a wing.

Jump an' spread out to let loose totally; go wild with abandon.

Key a close friend: *u.* 'im a mi key; key spar.

Kick the flavour of the moment, happening: *u.* DJ Shabba a kick.

Kinarkey a garishly made up woman.

Kirr-out light cuss word meaning to clear off.

Kotch 1. *(derog.)* to hang around, though unwelcome. **2.** to perch oneself in/on a small space: *u.* me can kotch ya; **3.** to hold open a door with a heavy object etc.: *u.* kotch de door deh fi me.

Kridel *(derog.)* an unattractive girl: *u.* back weh, kridel.

Kuh look at: *u.* kuh yuh to/*look at you too.*

Kulu-kulu abundant, plenty: *u.* de food kulu-kulu.

Expressions

Kick up rumpus to have a flaming good time.

Kill a sound to out-perform a rival DJ, sound, etc.

Kill me wid it give me more, usually of music or sex.

Labba-labba *(Ja. derog.)* to talk excessively: *u.* she too labba-labba.

Lamb's breath a more potent form of marijuana distinguished by its fluffy leaves in the mature stage.

Lang-gut gluttonous: *u.* what a lang-gut bway.

Let-off to give: *u.* let-off something, nuh/*give me something, please (begging).*

Level-vibes a salutation meaning everything is O.K.

Libatty rudeness: *u.* to tek libatty wid/*to be rude to.*

LET OFF SOME DOLLARS NUH STAR

YU NO SEE YU POCKET CAAN HOLD NO MORE

Foster

Lick 1. hit, blow: *u.* a bitch lick/*a devasting blow.* **2.** happening; the rage: *u.* a dat a de lick.

Lick it back rewind; start again from the top (musically): *u.* lick it back, selector.

Lick it dung to tear down.

Lick shot firing a gun or imitating its sound (done at the Dancehall as a mark of respect for the performing artiste).

Lick-out to speak out against: *u.* to lick out against racism.

Licky-licky *(derog)* a freeloading arse-kisser.

Liss Lisp: *u.* she 'av liss tongue.

Livity a healthy, positive attitude towards life.

Lizard lap sexual position.

Lookable attractive: *u.* she lookable.

Low-bite a person of the upper class with a taste for the common.

Luge huge; mega; massive.

EXPRESSIONS

Little-miss big young girl with Lolita type precocity.

Live-pon-y'eye-top to scrounge.

Lose-de-work to lose one's girlfriend.

Lullo-bump vulva/clitoris.

Maas 1. mask; conceal: *u.* maas yuh face/*conceal your face* **2.** money.

Macca 1. thorns: *u.* macca jook me **2.** wickedly good: *u.* de ting macca.

Madda herbal spiritualist; clairvoyant healer.

Main-squeeze one's lover: *u.* she's my main-squeeze.

Mampy fat, buxom woman.

Mange of negative behaviour, attitude etc.

Mannish water a soup made with a ram goat's head and feet, and flavoured with lots of spice, especially pepper.

Mash it an expression of encouragement: *u.* mash it, star/*break a leg.*

Mash-mout the appearance of the mouth without teeth: *u.* de mash mout bwoy.

Massive a large crowd; a group of friends (amount).

Matey **1.** a woman, female friend **2.** a rival: *u.* to banton yuh matey/*to go one up on one's rival.*

Matic automatic (usually of guns).

Mattrass someone, usually female who sleeps around.

Maw the oral or vaginal cavity: *u.* to look in someone's maw.

Mawgah extremely slim, thin: *u.* bwoy, yuh mawgah, eeh?/*boy, you are skinny!*

Men used as a singular word to mean a homosexual: *u.* dat bwoy is a men.

Merry-macka dancehall slang for America, transliterated it means 'merry but thorny'.

Mesh 1. to blend 2. well-dressed.

Mind 1. financial support: *u.* im nah mind 'im pickney dem/*he does not support his children* 2. attention: *u.* nuh pay her no mind.

Missa-man a term of respect not related to gangsterism.

Monkey lotion acid, thrown on someone so as to cause burning and disfiguration.

Monkey-money a small sum thought to be of no real value: *u.* me nuh have nuh use fi monkey-money.

Monster mega big, mega bad, extremely big, fantastic.

Motive what are your plans: *u.* weh de motive.

Mout to make fun of.

Mout-a-massey a chatterbox.

Mowly offensive odor: *u.* g'wey, you smell too mowly.

Mowly-aam rank body odour.

Mr Mention someone who is very popular.

Mud-up 1. the menstrual period 2. a general reference to one's state after intercourse 3. to be seen in the same outfit on more than one occasion.

Mule female incapable of conceiving.

Mungs amongst: *u.* mungs mi bredren.

Murdah an expression to describe something eye-catching or great, a wicked piece of music, etc.

My ting a girlfriend (user stating claim).

EXPRESSIONS

Madda-young-gal an obviously aging woman who clings passionately to things of youth.

Mix-up artist a mischief maker: *u.* dem people deh a mix-up artist.

Mass-yu-face Hide your face: *u.* mass yuh face cause yuh drop off a shape.

Nahsi dirty; filthy: *u.* yuh too nahsi/*you're too dirty*.

Nahsi-naygah relating to rudeness or coarseness in behaviour: *u.* mek de nahsi-naygah bwoy gwaan.

Name-bran of brand names; high fashion.

Natty 1. natty-dreadlocks 2. knotty.

Naygah *(derog.)* person, often used with 'dutty' or ol': *u.* me no business wid ol' naygah.

Nectar semen.

Nest home.

Niceness tender loving; good times.

Nie-nite (nine-night) a wake (usually held on the ninth night after someone's death). In terms of its application to the dancehall it refers to the 'death' of a sound.

Nite-Nurse 1. a woman who gives tender loving care to her man. 2. cocaine and its addictive qualities.

Nuff 1. plenty; abundant 2. presumptuous, conceited: *u.* yuh too nuff.

Nuff-respect a greeting; deference (embodies a greeting and deference, as one would greet a superior or a friend).

Nuh ready of a person thought not yet ready for the role he/she is playing, social or otherwise, also of fashion etc. which isn't quite right.

Nyah rastaman

Nyah-bingi a spiritual convention of the Rastafarian movement.

Nyam *(Ja. from Afr.)* to eat.

Nyamy-nyamy gluttonous: *u.* yuh too nyamy-nyamy.

EXPRESSIONS

Needle-eye poom-poom a tight vagina.

Neva see come see the new rich; easily impressed.

Obeah Jamaican black magic: *u.* to wuk obeah.

Official state of the art, recognized: *u.* a mi official dawta.

One-away one to one; intimate: *u.* a wi' check yuh one-away later.

Oneness unity, brotherhood: *u.* a oneness we a deal wid/*it's time for unity.*

EXPRESSIONS

Ol' bruck any and all items, of used clothing: *u.* me nuh wear ol' bruck.

Ol' bungle to look simply awful; decrepit: *u.* yu favour ol' bungle (also dutty bungle).

Ol' foot of older people.

Palaav to hang out; indulge oneself.

Par (to par with) to hang out with: *u.* me a0 par wid mi posse/*I'm hanging out with friends.*

Parados (usually of gambling) a last opportunity to recoup.

Parro paranoid, paronoia as a result of being stoned.

Patty a Jamaican meat pie.

Pawn to take hold of: *u.* if a ever pawn yuh/*don't let me take hold of you.*

Peggy a woman with sexual passion for a particular group of men (for example, one who sleeps only with policemen is known as a police peggy).

Penny to observe deeply: *u.* me a penny de vibes.

Pharmacist dealer in the illegal drug trade: *u.* 'im a big time pharmacist.

Pink-a-form enjoying the best of health, one's performance capacity etc.: *u.* 'im in pink-a-form.

Pirate 1. oppressors 2. musical (DJ).

Play-three the act of dying; death.

Poco (short for pocomania) a type of revivalist religion with its own style of songs and dance, whose impact is heavily felt in the dancehall.

Polish 'n' shine oral sex: *u.* she polish 'n' shine/*she indulges in oral sex.*

Politricks politics, usually implying dishonesty.

Poom-poom the vagina.

Pon on, upon.

Poop-a-lick somersault: *u.* to kin poop-a-lick/*to do a somersault.*

Pop-off the act of reaching for ones' firearm.

Pop-style to affect airs: *u.* what a way she ah pop-style.

Poppy-show someone who takes him/herself seriously but is regarded only as amusing by others; a foolishly silly person.

Posse entourage: *u.* uptown posse.

Post (to post someone) not showing up for an appointment: *u.* a post de bwoy.

Pot-cover-love lesbianism: *u.* me nuh deal wid de pot-cover-love.

Potion amount, numbers etc., of large quantities: *u.* a potion a girls.

Powder-puff a very special woman: *u.* she a mi powder-puff.

Prekkeh 1. to allow oneself to be used as a go-for: *u.* 'im a everybody prekkeh **2.** a scandalous happening: *u.* what a prekkeh!

Prentice *(Eng. apprentice)* young associate; protegé.

Progressive rope neck tie (sign of upward mobility).

Pronto *(Sp.)* at once; immediately.

Punaani the vagina: *u.* me luv punaani bad.

Push-up presumptuous: *u.* yuh too push-up.

Pussy-bully a male who is very sexually active; sex enthusiast.

Pussy-printer form-hugging shorts. Type of shorts worn so tight it actually shows off the shape of the pubic area.

Put-on to affect airs.

Putus a term of endearment: *u.* hi, putus.

Quaabs socially equal: *u.* we nuh quaabs/*we are not social equals.*

Quashie idiot.

Raasing a thorough thrashing: *u.* give de bwoy a raasing

Race up to chase away: *u.* race up de bwoy.

Ragamuffin dancehall title of respect.

Ram having a capacity crowd: *u.* de place ram/*the venue is packed.*

Ratchet a pocket knife which when modified operates like a switchblade.

Raw hungry: *u.* me raw/*I'm very hungry.*

Raw-chaw 1. the naked truth 2. vulgar, unadulterated.

Reader a seer; fortune teller: *u.* me a go to the reader for a read-up.

Red 1. an awful sate of affairs: *u.* things red 2. stoned.

Red-eye covetous: *u.* she red-eye, yuh see/*she's very covetous.*

Renk 1. extremely insolent, impolite or rude: *u.* what a renk bwoy 2. a pungent, foul odour.

Renking meat vagina.

Rep reputation: *u.* don't mess with my rep.

Request to a dedication (musical): *u.* request to Polly.

Respect dancehall greeting.

Rev-out prematurely past one's sexual prime.

Rightid being sensible; sane: *u.* she not rightid/ *she's a bit crazy.*

Rings firearms: *u.* go fi yuh rings/*reach for your firearm.*

Risto of the upper class.

Rope-in an invitation to participate; to include.

Rough-neck ragamuffin.

Rub a slow sensuos dance punctuated by pelvic thrusts and grinds.

Rub-a-dub heavy instrumental music, also type of dance.

Rub-a-dub soldier dancehall enthusiast.

Rum-head alcoholic.

Run belly to cause diarrhoea: *u.* stale po'k wi' run yuh belly.

Run hot 1. be in demand 2. wanted by the police: *u.* John a run hot/*John is wanted* 3. prolonged intercourse.

Run-dung 1. to chase after. 2. a Jamaican meal (a stew) prepared from salted mackerel, coconut milk and assorted spices.

Running-belly diarrhoea: *u.* 'im 'ave a bad running-belly.

Ruption a disturbance.

Rush 1. to attack someone **2.** to be the centre of attention: *u.* dem a rush me.

EXPRESSIONS

Ramp wid to play around (usuallyused in the negative): *u.* me don't ramp wid food/*I'm a serious eater.*

Rub a sentence to do time: *u.* Tom a rub a sentence/*Tom is doing time.*

Run a boat the act of pooling resources to afford and prepare a meal; cooking: *u.* we a go run a boat.

Saaf drinks bottled soda: *u.* buy me a saaf drinks, nuh.

Salad (especially of sport) be made to look foolish; to be taken in: *u.* yuh buy a salad/*you're stuck with a lemon.*

Salt ill fortune; spate of hard luck; time when nothing seems to go right: *u.* t'ings well salt.

Samfie *(Ja.)* pull a confidence trick: *u.* to samfie someone.

Sample 1. unique 2. *(derog.)* mild mannered male: *u.* yuh a sample.

Saps an ineffective male: *u.* me nuh deal wid saps.

Satta A command to stay put.

Screechy to move stealthily.

Screw to sport an intimidatory scowl, showing one's displeasure.

Seh 1. say *u.* weh yuh a seh/*what's happening, what are you saying* 2. that: *u.* him tell me seh she gawn.

Seh one to look good (of a female): *u.* gal, yuh a seh one.

Seh-seh seh-seh gossip: *u.* me nuh mix up eena seh-seh seh-seh.

Selector the nonperforming D.J. who selects records, operates turntables, and plays records.

Sensemilla high grade seedless marijuana grown in the mountain regions of the Jamaican countryside.

Sess sensemilla.

Set the various components characterized by massive boxes, giant speakers that provide the music for dancehall.

Shaka an unattractive or ugly person.

Shake to move on: *u.* I man a shake de spot.

Sheg-up 1. a dirty attitude: *u.* 'im sheg up/*he has a nasty attitude* **2.** to make a mess of: *u.* 'im sheg-up de plan.

Shine oral sex: *u.* she polish 'n' shine/*she practises oral sex.*

Shine-eye gal a material girl.

Shiners lamé or sparkly fabrics: *u.* to dress up in shiners.

Shit general term for illegal drugs (*marijuana not included*): u. a coulda use some shit/*I need a fix.*

Shock 'n' sting far out (of fashion, music).

Shock-out (of appearance) anything fabulous or eye catching: *u.* de car a shock-out/*it's eye catching.*

Shoot a person who is shooting is infected with V.D.: *u.* de gal a shoot.

Silver-bangle handcuffs: *u.* me nuh wan' wear nuh silver bangle.

Sing-jay a DJ who combines singing with DJing.

Skank 1. type of dance 2. to con someone.

Skin teet to laugh at, to joke with someone.

Skin-out 1. to carry-on; enjoy oneself 2. sexual abandonment.

Skin-up to be on friendly terms: *u.* me no skin-up wid 'im.

Skull to play traunt: *u.* yuh skull too much.

Skylark irresponsible behaviour; to play the fool.

Slabbah-slabbah the state of being grossly overweight; a fat individual: *u.* a one slabbah-slabbah gal.

Slackness vulgarity.

Sling-shot skimpy underwear.

Smaddy someone: *u.* yuh fava smaddy me know.

So till very, beyond words: *u.* 'im ugly so till/ *He's indescribably ugly.*

So-so only: *u.* a so-so drinks 'im gi' me/*He gave·me only a drink.*

Sound-systems *see* set.

Spar friend: *u.* wha' happen, spar?

Sparring-partner buddy, friend: *u.* him a mi sparring partner.

Speng a type of strutting walk characterised by an intense slouching of the shoulder, accompanied by buttoning up of one's collar; a toughie.

Spliff a marijuana joint: *u.* to smoke a spliff.

Spread-out to let oneself go; let loose.

Star a salutation: *u.* hail, star.

Sting the flavour of the moment; breath taking: *u.* a dat a sting.

Stone potion used to prolong a man's sexual performance.

Stoosh false, sophisticated: *u.* she gwaan stoosh.

Stoshus posh, upper crust, sophisticated.

Sud-up state after sexual intercourse *u. de gal sud-up.*

Switch usually someone who was supposedly a heterosexual who's now thought to be a homosexual: *u.* de bwoy switch.

EXPRESSIONS

S the spot to take one's leave; departure: *u.* me a s the spot.

Season breast women masturbate then smear their fluids over their breasts. When later, as part of foreplay, the unsuspecting man licks, sucks, or nibbles on these tits he's said to be having season breasts.

Shoot the bishop nocturnal emmission; masturbation.

Tallawah effective, strong: *u.* me little but me tallawah.

Tampi marijuana.

Tan stay: *u.* tan yah so till me come/*wait here until I return.*

Tegehreg a woman prone to brawling.

Tekeesha gold-digger.

Telegram-carrier term used (by women) to describe men with no sexual staying power: *u.* de bwoy a telegram carrier.

Tician politicians; political activist: *u.* me nuh check fi tician.

Ticky-ticky inconsequential; small timer.

Tool firearm; gun: *u.* to walk wid one's tool.

Topanaris of the upper class: *u.* she a topanaris, mi love.

Trace verbal abuse; a cussing out: *u.* to trace someone.

Trailer-load a large quantity; huge: *u.* trailer-load a girls deh a de dance.

Trample to have sexual intercourse: *u.* to trample de beef.

Trampooze out on the town: *u.* to trampooze wid mi bredren.

Tranquillo remain calm; stay cool.

Trash well-dressed.

Truss 1. credit, loan **2.** have confidence: *u.* me nuh truss dem/*I have no confidence in them.*

Tun turn.

Turbo-charged a very attractive, well-proportioned woman.

Turfite veteran; seasoned: *u.* dancehall turfite/ *regular dance patron.*

Tyad unattractive, overused: *u.* dis ol' tyad frock.

EXPRESSIONS

Tan-pon-it-long sexual staying power; male prowess.

Tan-so-back do not retaliate; chill; refrain from taking aggressive action.

Tan-tudy stand still; be cool.

Tear-it-down a smashing performance.

Things curry everything is o.k.; there's no need to worry.

Trash 'n' ready well dressed and ready to go: *u.* 'im look trash 'n' ready.

Unu all of you; everyone: *u.* unu ready yet?/*are you all ready?*

Up-front straight forward; no room for deceit.

Up-fullness clean, healthy living; straight-forwardness.

Vampire corporate business; government; the Establishment.

Vampire-bag sanitary pad: *u.* she a wear 'ar vampire-bag.

Vanity wealth; things material.

Vank **1.** to dismiss someone. **2.** to die: *u.* im vank/*he died.*

Veggie-meat 1. available young women **2.** virgin.

Version instrumental side of a 45 record: *u.* lick back de version.

Vibe-out to chill out; to take a break.

Vibes vibrations; positive energy flow.

Viking cheats; oppressors (see vampire).

EXPRESSIONS

Visa-body a desired body; object of lust.

Wack a large sum of money.

Wagga-wagga 1. over abundance **2.** flabby.

Walk (as in orange-walk) grove.

Wanga-gut greedy; gluttonous: *u.* 'im is a wanga-gut.

Wassy wild; very good: *u.* de music well wassy.

Wee-wee urine.

Weed marijuana

Weh 1. what: *u.* a weh you wan'/*what do you want?* 2. where: *u.* weh she deh/*where is she?*

White-liver nymphomania: *u.* de gal 'ave white liver.

Wild 1. philandering 2. word of approval, praise, etc.

Wine sexual gyration; to dance in a sexually suggestive and provocative manner.

Winery sexual prowess.

Worries conflict; problems: *u.* worries eena de dance/*there's conflict in the dance.*

Wrinch to sport a scowl (see screw).

Wuk 1. work 2. a relationship: *u.* to lose de wuk/*to lose one's girl.*

EXPRESSIONS

Watch-it-man move on.

What a way expression of degree: *u.* what a way she pretty/*how pretty she is!*

Wicked-wassy 'n' wild extraordinary, super 'bad'.

X amount countless

Yagga-yagga behaving in an unbecoming way.

Yahso here; location: *u.* a yahso we deh/*here is where we are.*

Yardie a Jamaican residing overseas: *u.* yardie, weh yuh a seh?/*fellow countryman, what's happening?*

Y'eye eye.

Yuh see very: *u.* she fat, yuh see/*she's very fat.*

Yuntry slang for country, rural area: *u.* yountry bwoy/*country bwoy.*

Yush hush; be cool: *u.* yush an tek in de music/*hush and listen to the music.*

Zoo a very unattractive person: *u.* gwaan yuh look like zoo/*you're very unattractive.*

Zutupeck an unattractive female: *u,* ol' zutupeck.

SWEARING... DANCEHALL STYLE
"Badwuds"

Swearing in the Dancehall is no less a colour-ful activity than any other Dancehall activity. What is interesting however, is that the Jamaican 'badwud' is so commonplace in everyday con-versation that it is only by amplification that they become potent.

Example: "Raas" is a fairly commonplace 'badwud' to be found in the daily vocabulary of most Jamaicans, so too are "bombo" (which is almost invariably used with "claat") and "fockin". However, by themselves these words as single entities are quite mundane and lacking in the 'blood and fire' an aggrieved individual would be wanting to put over. The effect is then achieved by combining (say) "bombo-raas-claat" to produce the vitriolic fire and brimstone effect.

As shown, it is by the process of amplifica-tion which further coarsens 'ordinary' badwuds to give them graphic meaning, and convey a sense of dread. The short list below provides a compact look at the vocabulary – the main words and their possible combinations.

Blood + claat	*Raas* + claat
hole	hole

Bombo + brush	*Dutty* + blood-claat
claat	bombo-claat
(sanitary pad)	pussy-claat
hole	pussy-hole
(vagina)	raas-claat
tongue	raas-hole
(clitoris)	bombo-raas-claat

Pussy + claat
hole

N.B. Any and all combinations are possible, and if the use of any 'badwud' or any of the combinations is prefaced by: "Kiss-out mi" then you are at the summit from which such vitriol springs, and if you are the individual being addressed, be under no illusions, you have caused offence, anger, etc., and you are being truly "blessed".

Caution: These badwuds are viewed as being so offensive that their use can, and often does, lead to heated arguments, fights and bodily harm.

Do **not** use them unless you are very confident that you know (a) the company you are in and (b) the true impression these words convey.

DANCEHALL POTIONS

The premiere drink(s) of the dance is any malt-based alcoholic bottled drink, as it is widely thought that these beverages contribute to the enhancement of one's sexual abilities. It is natural that the macho environment lends itself to promoting a culture of organic drinks, both alcoholic and non-alcoholic, which reportedly act as sexual enhancers. Some herbal-based drinks are believed to be healthy and to improve stamina, therby producing the 'tan-pon-it-long' effect.

Alcoholic

STEEL-BOTTOM
1 bottle Jamaican Red Stripe beer
2 oz white overproof rum

Sip about two ounces of the Red Stripe from the bottle then pour the overproof rum into the remaining beer.
Shake well.

FRONT-END LIFTER
1 bottle Dragon stout
1 raw egg
1 bottle Red Label wine

Pour all above ingredients into a container (mixer), shake well.

Non-Alcoholic

MAGNUM
1 lb Irish moss
1/2 lb linseed
1/4 lb gummerbit

Cook all three until liquid achieves a pasty texture. Allow to cool. Strain, then add:

2 oz rum
2 oz vanilla
1 oz grated nutmeg
1 bottle Dragon stout
1/4 oz fresh liquified peanuts
6 whipped eggs.

Add milk and sugar to taste.

STRONG-BACK

1 quart cooked and strained Irish moss
6 oz uncooked oats
4 oz liquified peanuts
6 oz broth made from the 'strong back'
    plant
6 oz liquified ripe paw-paw (papaya)
1 or more bottles Dragon stout
a pinch of salt.

Combine all the above ingredients, add honey to taste.

ROOTS

A visit to the market is necessary where a herbalist will have prepackaged portions of:
Chainey-root
Bridal-wisp
Sarsiparilla
Strong-back
Wood-root
Arrow-root

One now needs a cauldron to cook all the above ingredients for at least two hours. When cooked, strain and allow to cool. Add molasses to taste.

PEP-UP
1 quart cooked and strained Irish moss
3 bottles Dragon stout
10 oz Red Label wine
6 oz liquified green corn

Combine the above ingredients, add milk, vanilla and honey to taste.

Note: The recipes and method of preparation vary from person to person, but basically the ingredients remain the same, except in rural areas and at some corporate area venues where a marijuana broth is added to the non-alcoholic drinks to "spice it up".

MONEY MATTERS

The term "money" is almost never used in the environment of the Dancehall. Instead, in the case of local denomination currency, etc., a series of colour codes, buzz-words, or images of national personalities which appear on notes are used to denote the sum intended.

Listed below are a number of prevailing terminologies used to denote not just currency but denomination as well as nationality.

General Terms for Money

Collateral	Maas
Backative	Change
Corn	Borrows
Dunsie	Breads

Foreign Currency

Local tender	Hard currency

N.B. These two terms have arisen, and apply to currencies such as the US Dollar; Pound Sterling; and the Deutsche Mark, owing to the weakness of the Jamaican Dollar.

Jamaican Currency

The bills are identified through various types of coding, which include:

(a) colour,

(b) the images which appear on them,

(c) words and or phrases; names, etc.

CONCORDE: $100.00 (so named because of the speed or ease with which it 'disappears').

SAM SHARPE: $50.00 (so called because of the image of the Jamaican National Hero that appears thereon).

BLOOD-MONEY: $20.00 (so called because of the primary red colour of the note).

PAPER-MONEY: any sum thought to be insignificant; inappropriate etc.

NUMBERS AND THEIR MEANING

'Drop-pan' has always been a part of the Jamaican experience, as this illegal numbers game, with its relatively low stake, and correspondingly high return, has been and continues to be a source of income for many.

The game, which is played using numbers from one (1) to thirty-six (36), has developed a coded structure wherein numbers have meanings, in order that participants can 'read the play'. Some of these numbers have become entrenched in the vocabulary as their coded nature allows for communication not necessarily understood outside of the ranks of the ardent Dancehall 'turfite', or the drop-pan player.

Given below is a list of numbers one is more likely to hear in the Dancehall environment and their approximate meanings:

2   Homosexual (batty-bwoy)
3   Death (*u.* to play three)
4   Blood
5   Thief
7   Married-woman
13   Police (Babylon)

14 Mouth (*u.* mout-a-massey/chatter-box)
16 Young girl (virgin)
17 Chinese (*u.* Chiney-man)
20 Illness
21 A whore
25 A crowd
27 Fire
32 Gold
36 An old woman

DANCING – DANCEHALL "STYLEE"

'To step it in a Dancehall style' is one of the more attractive aspects of the Dancehall culture. As with the speech, Dancehall dances keep pace with their environment and consequently are constantly changing.

The following list should serve to provide a "functioning" knowledge of the more popular dances to date.

The Butterfly	Water-pumpy
The Bogle	The Batty-rider
Della-move	Skin-out
Cool 'n' deadly	The Duck
Bubbling	Slide 'n' wine
Jockey fashion	

GHETTO VIBES

Since Bob Marley's *Trench Town Rock*, the Jamaican urban ghetto has continued playing its central role in the evolution of Jamaican music. In more recent times a number of these communities have come to assume a more prominent role in the lyrics of the music owing to the number of 'posses' they have spawned and the international attention and notoriety which these posses have created.

Set below is a short list of the more prominent of these communities, and the "posses" they have nurtured.

COMMUNITIES	POSSES
Trench Town	
Waterhouse	Firehouse
Whitehall	
Rema	
Tivoli Gardens	Shower (local)
Wareika Hill	Warikers
Dunkirk	
Southside	
Mall Road	Mawlers
Tel-Aviv	Soldiers

Overseas Posses

HOT STEPPERS

Miami based, originate from the South-side area of Kingston.

SHOWER

Operate primarily in New York, Miami, Washington and other major US cities. Origins Tivoli Gardens in Western Kingston.

SPANGLERS

Roots lie in Kingston's Arnett Gardens. Operate in New York, Miami, Atlanta, Philadelphia, and other US cities and in Toronto, Canada.

RENKERS

A collection of various gang members out of Jamaica who banded together in the US. Operate the length and breadth of the US and in Toronto.

ABOUT THE RESEARCHER/COMPILER

Chester Francis-Jackson is one of Jamaica's leading publicists and social writers. He has written extensively for both national and international publications. He is the founding publisher/editorial director of the monthly magazine *Profile*, and also the chairman/managing director of the publicity and image consultancy firm Images and Profiles. He was educated in North America and the Caribbean.

A resident of Jamaica, he is currently completing work on two novels – *Low Life in High Places,* and *Concentric Circles.*